Reading
Sounder

THE ENGAGED READER

THE ENGAGED READER

Reading
Sounder

Pamela Loos

CHELSEA HOUSE
PUBLISHERS
A Haights Cross Communications ® Company ®
Philadelphia

CHELSEA HOUSE PUBLISHERS

VP, NEW PRODUCT DEVELOPMENT Sally Cheney
DIRECTOR OF PRODUCTION Kim Shinners
CREATIVE MANAGER Takeshi Takahashi
MANUFACTURING MANAGER Diann Grasse

Staff for READING SOUNDER

EDITOR Matt Uhler
PHOTO EDITOR Sarah Bloom
PRODUCTION EDITOR Bonnie Cohen
EDITORIAL ASSISTANT Sarah Sharpless
SERIES DESIGNER Takeshi Takahashi
COVER DESIGNER Takeshi Takahashi
LAYOUT EJB Publishing Services

A Haights Cross Communications ✦ Company ®

www.chelseahouse.com

First Printing

9 8 7 6 5 4 3 2 1

Library of Congress Cataloging-in-Publication Data
Loos, Pamela.
  Reading Sounder / Pamela Loos.
    p. cm. — (The engaged reader)
  Includes bibliographical references and index.
  ISBN 0-7910-8833-2
1. Armstrong, William Howard, 1914- Sounder—Juvenile literature. 2.
African American families in literature—Juvenile literature. 3. Dogs in litera-
ture—Juvenile literature. 4. Boys in literature—Juvenile literature. 5. Poor in
literature—Juvenile literature. I. Title. II. Series.
  PS3551.R483S6835 2005
  813'.54—dc22

                                    2005010300

Table of Contents

Contexts

OFTEN READERS WANT INFORMATION about the author of a book that they are planning to read. Readers feel it may give them insight into why the author wrote the work and/or that it may show the author's experience with the topic he or she wrote about. Readers need to be reminded, however, that writers of fiction are creating their works not only out of their experiences but also out of their imaginations. Just because, for example, a book is written in the first person, written from the perspective of "I," we cannot assume that the author is the speaker or narrator. "I" can be a fictional narrator that the author has created.

In the case of William H. Armstrong, the author of *Sounder*, it is interesting to know that he was born in Virginia in 1914 and that his father was a farmer. This indicates that he knew people who lived during the time shortly after the Civil War in the United States, the time period that *Sounder* is set in. Also, his experience living on a farm would come in handy when writing *Sounder*, since the family in *Sounder* lives on a farm. Armstrong went to college and graduate school in Virginia and was married in 1943 to Martha Stone Street Williams. In 1945, he became a history teacher at Kent School in Kent, Connecticut. Obviously, then, he values education, a key value of the main character in *Sounder* as well.

Armstrong began by writing nonfiction books, some of which were self-improvement books; then, in 1969 when *Sounder* was published, he started writing fiction as well as nonfiction. *Sounder* was immediately popular when it was released and remains Armstrong's most popular book to this day. It won the Newbery Medal and other awards. In 1972, it was made into a movie.

Considering that the book tells the plight of a young black boy and his poor family, it might at first seem curious to find out that Armstrong himself is not a black man. While such a situation is unusual, other authors have put themselves in similar situations, writing a book from the perspective of a boy when they are not male, for example. Yet, when *Sounder* was published, some critics were upset that Armstrong was writing about a black experience without being black. Armstrong responded that he was writing about the universal problem of poverty and how it is allowed to persist; he said that the people in the novel do not necessarily have to be black.

Actually, considering when Armstrong's book was

published, it is not so surprising that he was criticized for writing a book about blacks without being black himself. The book was published in 1969, not long after major changes began taking place in the United States in regard to civil rights for blacks. While the Civil Rights Bill of 1957 was in place, it proved ineffective, leaving blacks the victims of prejudice that expressed itself in numerous ways, such as the "separate but equal" status that existed for blacks in much of the South. Under this system, blacks were separated from whites on buses, in schools, in restaurants, and in nearly every arena of daily life. Not only were they separated, but, it was realized, what they were receiving was nearly never equal to—often below—what the whites were receiving.

In the 1960s, a massive movement of protests ensued, with such men as Reverend Martin Luther King Jr. and Thurgood Marshall leading the way. In 1963, about 200,000 protestors met in Washington, D.C. New legislation with substance was finally passed—the Civil Rights Act of 1964. It made discrimination illegal and allowed federal funds to be withheld from schools that were still segregated.

By 1969, then, when *Sounder* was published, some people were sensitive about the true black voice being heard. Perhaps the events of the 1960s inspired Armstrong to write *Sounder* in an attempt to give voice to the discriminated. Although the action in *Sounder* takes place after the Civil War period, the discrimination of that period was still too real even in the 1960s, nearly 100 years after the Civil War.

The 1960s also was a time of revolution in arenas other than civil rights. People rebelled against the staid 1950s, when everyone had seemed willing to accept a more standardized, restricted, and sanitized lifestyle. In the

1960s protests took place against the government for its involvement in Vietnam, against society for its treatment of women and minorities, against parents for their lack of understanding of the new long-haired, blue jean-wearing, rock 'n' roll-listening teenagers. Peace symbols appeared all over. Such an atmosphere could readily provoke an author to publish a book like *Sounder*, which warns that society needs to change.

Before reading *Sounder*, what would be helpful to know about the time period covered in the book? The events in the book take place in the United States not long after the end of the Civil War. The South, which had fought with great determination during the war to keep slavery, lost the war and was left wondering how its plantations would survive without free labor. Landowners needed help and former slaves, while skilled at farm work, had no money to start their own farms. In response to these needs, there developed a system called sharecropping, where a landowner would rent small cabins to farm workers, who

ON YOUR OWN
ACTIVITY #1

We learn that *Sounder* is based on stories that an old teacher told to William Armstrong. We know, too, that the book was published in 1969 and that the 1960s made up a tumultuous era that brought about various societal changes. Talk to some people who lived during the 1960s and ask them to tell you some interesting stories about that time. Write down your favorite one. While the events in *Sounder* take place much earlier than the 1960s, as you read the book, think about what might have needed to happen in the post-Civil War era for change to truly occur and for injustice to be removed.

received a percentage of the harvested crops in return for their labor on the farm.

While families that had been slaves were no longer controlled and brutalized by their owners, they still endured great hardships. When the crop harvest was poor, these families suffered, whereas when they had been slaves, their owners looked out for them, intent on preserving their investment. Additionally, such black farmers still endured hardships as a result of intense prejudice that was not wiped away with the end of the war.

In light of that background, let's look more closely at *Sounder*. On the front cover of the Harper Trophy edition, we see a young black boy in overalls with a hunting dog sitting close to him. Since they are sitting so closely, we assume they have a good relationship. The dog and the boy are both looking in different directions. The dog appears fully alert, like a hunting dog ready for the chase, while the boy is looking off to the other side. Is he lost in his thoughts? Worried about something? It is hard to tell. Perhaps the dog is alert not just because he is a hunter but because he is expectant of something or on the lookout to keep his friend safe.

When we look at other versions of the front cover, we see that the earliest cover was done by the illustrator who did the artwork that appeared inside the first edition. On the illustrator's cover, the dog and the boy are both pictured, again looking in different directions, but the boy is looking toward us, the readers, with a rather forlorn look.

On another cover version, the dog appears by himself, looking into the distance, with his back facing the reader. There is something about the way we see his head and back, sort of as one oblong shape, that almost could make us think the shape is that of a person with his back to us.

This makes us think of the dog as more human. Since the title of the book is the dog's name, which gives the dog prominence, it might also be logical to assume that the dog does have some seemingly human qualities. On the front cover, there also is the seal showing that the book has won the prestigious Newbery Award, again a positive sign that the book is a good one.

On the back cover, we get a brief explanation of the book's contents. We read that the book is "a landmark in children's literature," which certainly makes it sound like it must be a good book. We see that the book focuses on the boy, who's poor and living in the South in the nineteenth century. The boy's father is a sharecropper who has been struggling to find food for his family but has been unsuccessful at hunting with the family dog, Sounder. Although good food is cooking in the kitchen one morning, "an angry sheriff" appears later that same night. We read that the boy's life "will never be the same."

From this we get a bit more information on what the book is about. Now we know that the boy is poor and living in the South more than a hundred years ago. The boy's family apparently is quite poor, since the father must go out in search of food for them. Unfortunately, just when it

ON YOUR OWN
ACTIVITY #2

From the back cover, we learn that *Sounder* involves an "angry sheriff," and we see the ominous jail in an illustration inside. Have you read any books or seen any movies where the people in authority did not treat everyone else fairly? What happened as a result of the injustice?

seems that luck has turned in the family's favor, an angry sheriff appears at the family's home. Knowing that he is angry, we assume that the boy's life probably is going to be changed for the worse.

On the back cover, there are also a few quotes from reviewers. One calls the book a "rarely beautiful, understated novel. An extraordinarily sensitive book." This prepares us that the story is told in an exceptional manner. Similarly, another quote on the back cover calls the book "powerfully moving."

Inside, there is a page of more quotes from reviews. Here we get a stronger impression of the pain in the book. We read that the book is grim and tragic, full of "cruelty, loneliness, and silent suffering." Before the book starts, there is also a page with a quote: "A man keeps, like his love, his courage dark." The quote is by Antoine de Saint Exupéry. Again, there is an ominous tone here. Apparently courage will be necessary in the story, but the true man doesn't have to boldly display it, we are told. We wonder if this is referring to the boy, to his father, or to someone else.

In the Author's Note, Armstrong states that *Sounder* is inspired by his memories of his first teacher, who told him stories from Aesop, the Greek fable author; from the Old Testament of the Bible; and from the Ancient Greek writer Homer. The teacher, a black man, also told him stories from his own life.

Narrative Technique

AN AUTHOR'S NARRATIVE technique refers to how his or her story is told and who is the narrator doing the telling. In *Sounder*, the story is told by a narrator writing primarily from the boy's perspective. We learn everything as the boy does and the narrator can also go inside the boy's mind and tell us what he is thinking or feeling. This type of narration, or method of telling the story, is called third-person narration.

Look, for example, at the description after Sounder is shot: "Sounder lay still in the road. The boy wanted to cry; he wanted to run to Sounder. His stomach felt sick. He didn't want to see

Sounder. He fell to his knees at the woodpile."[1] In this passage, the narrator uses phrases such as "the boy wanted to cry" or "he wanted to run." When a narrator uses such words as "he," "they," or "she," it indicates that the work is in the third person. (When an author uses "I," this means that the work is written in the first person.)

Sounder is written in the third person and from a limited point of view—that of the boy. In other instances, a book may be written in the third person, yet the narrator tells us what each character, not just one character, is thinking or feeling; in this case, the narration is "third-person omniscient." *Omniscient* refers to knowing everything; the third-person omniscient narrator knows everything that has happened or is happening to all the characters; this type of narrator knows all the characters' thoughts and feelings.

A key element the author uses in *Sounder* to make the reader feel that this is the boy's story is the language—the language sounds like language the boy would use. For example, none of the sentences are overly complex; this is what we would expect from someone who is young.

Another important factor about the narrative technique in

ON YOUR OWN
ACTIVITY #3

Sounder is told in the third person and from the boy's perspective. How would the story be different if the narration was third-person omniscient, that is, if the author also delved inside the thoughts of other characters, such as the mother, father, or teacher? Certainly readers would learn more than they do now, but there would be things lost by not having all of the attention focused on the boy. What would be lost?

Sounder is revealed in the Author's Note at the beginning of the book. Here, Armstrong tells us that when he was young, a gray-haired black teacher taught him to read. The teacher worked for his father after school and in the summers, and after doing this work, he would teach the young Armstrong. Then, after the lessons, he would tell stories from "Aesop, the Old Testament, Homer, and history." While the teacher usually did not talk about himself, one night he told the boy the story of *Sounder*. "It is the black man's story, not mine. It was not from Aesop, the Old Testament, or Homer. It was history—*his* history." The book, then, is not a story that the author made up, but is based on his teacher's own life. Because of this, the events in the book are perhaps even more disturbing but also more inspiring because they are based on a real person's life.

THE USE OF STORIES

The use of stories is an important element of the narrative technique in *Sounder*. Within the overall story of the book, many brief stories are told as well. The mother is the main character that relates these stories. The boy depends on her to tell him stories so he doesn't feel so lonely, but the stories serve another purpose beyond this. Almost all of the stories the mother tells are stories from the Bible. To her, they are an important part of her faith and they have important messages to convey. Obviously, she hopes to instill a strong faith in her son as well.

Aside from the fact that all of the stories the mother tells are Bible stories, most of them also have basically the same theme: someone is in trouble and God helps the person. One of the most broad-ranging stories the mother tells is the story of the flood, which, according to the Christian faith, was sent to wipe away all evil. The message is that

God will punish evil and reward good. Another Bible tale is about Lazarus, who God brings back from the dead. We can tell that the boy wants to believe in the stories and apply them to his life when he says to himself that maybe Sounder will come back from the dead like Lazarus did.

A similar Bible story that the mother tells is about God parting the sea so the Jewish people can escape from Egypt. Also, when the boy worries about his father, who is in jail, his mother tells the story of three jailed men who were thrown into an oven as big as a furnace but were saved by the Lord. When the door to the oven was opened, the flames had been quenched and the three men were singing about the Lord and his cool water. The boy thinks to himself that no oven could be big enough to fit three men; perhaps this is a sign of his own growing up and thinking for himself. The boy especially likes the story of Joseph, who was enslaved and then imprisoned but ends up a powerful man. When the boy argues with his mother to let him search for his father, he reminds her that in the Bible stories many people go on journeys and all find what they are looking for in the end.

On the road, searching for his father, the boy realizes that he's memorized his mother's stories and that he appreciates how the endings always work out well and how the characters are never afraid. At one point on the road at night, he hears the wind in the top of trees and is reminded of the Bible story of King David. According to the story, the Lord tells David that when he hears the wind in the treetops, it is a sign that the Lord is there, ready to fight on his side, and that David's army will win. The boy in *Sounder* listens, imagines David's army, and "wasn't afraid with David near." As he falls asleep, he thinks he sees a lantern far off in the woods and thinks he hears Sounder's great voice.

The Bible stories comfort the boy, but on the road as he reads stray newspaper articles and tries to put them together to make new stories, he realizes they "never came out right" and made him more afraid. There is a direct comparison here, then, between the comfort of the Bible stories and the dissatisfaction and fear the newspaper stories provoke. In the process of searching for his father, the boy has pushed himself into the real world and its unpleasant news. Even though his mother is not on the road with him, he calls upon her stories to comfort him. The information in the newspapers reports real events, which, like his life so far, prove to be disturbing. The boy stays attached to the Bible stories, which offer the promise of something better.

Aside from Bible stories and newspaper articles, the big book that the boy finds in the trash serves as another way to tell a story or comment about life. The book is described as "a book of stories about what people think. There were titles such as Cruelty, Excellent Men, Education, Cripples, Justice, and many others."[2] The book is actually a book of essays, which are commentaries about different subjects, but since the boy hasn't had much experience with books or reading at this point, he assumes the book contains stories.

The boy mentions a few of the book's topics, and we can see that these are not purely chosen by chance but that all relate to the boy's own life. Cruelty and justice certainly are monumental realities in the boy's life, as he and his family experience the cruelty and questionable justice surrounding his father's arrest and he sees other examples of cruelty in his travels as well. "Excellent Men" also seems an appropriate topic for the boy to read about since he admires his father and the people in the Bible stories, as well as the teacher he meets later, but he has met many far-from-excellent men as well. Education certainly is another timely topic from the book, since the boy is intent on getting an education and finally does at the end of the book.

The first part of the book that the boy tries to read is a section on cruelty. The essay says that cowardice is what actually is behind cruelty and that those who treat others horribly are almost always weak. It gives the example that wolves and bears go after dead things, implying that they, and men like them, are too weak and too lacking in courage to take on a real challenge. The boy reads the book aloud to himself, and we get to hear its exact words. We, too, can draw our own conclusions. The boy knows about cruelty, since he has encountered the cruel sheriff and his men as well as the man at the jail. According to the essay in the book, these men are actually weak and cowardly, a contrast to the boy and his family, who stand out for their strength and determination even in the most challenging situations. The boy is frustrated because he reads the essay and doesn't understand it, but we can see that if he does learn to read better, the book will be of great value to him.

The book found in the trash also provides a message later, when the boy meets the teacher and the teacher sees what he is carrying. The teacher knows the book and says that few people read it, even though they should. This shows us the teacher's perspective—that the world needs people to read such essays so it can become a better place.

The teacher bandages the boy's injured hand and says he will read to the boy from the book, but instead he starts to tell the boy about one of the stories. He tells the boy it is about a king who wants to buy a horse from his soldier and who asks what the soldier would like in return—money or a kingdom, perhaps. The soldier says he would not sell his horse for money or exchange it for a kingdom but that he would give it freely to a friend. The teacher realizes he's told the boy the whole story and doesn't need to read it, and the boy responds, "You've been a powerful good friend to take me in like this. My fingers don't hurt no more."[3]

The boy's response is revealing for a few reasons. First, it shows what a kind, appreciative boy he is. He's been so impressed with the teacher and the teacher's kindness, he literally feels like he's had his wounds healed. Less directly, the boy's response shows that he has completely understood the point of the story—that friendship is so important that it has more value than any amount of money or great power. The fact that the teacher told him the story instead of reading it made it easier for the boy to understand, but the fact that the boy so readily understood its point shows that the book and others like it will help the boy grow once he can read them himself.

This section of *Sounder* is also important because the teacher is the first kind person the boy has met outside his family. The fact that the teacher relates the tale about friendship indicates his own perspective on life and that he can be a valuable person for helping the boy. The teacher, then, can add on to the lessons the boy's mother has tried to teach him with the Bible stories. The selections in the book the boy has found, however, won't be like the stories his mother tells him that all have happy endings.

The book of essays is also quoted at the end of *Sounder*. At that point, the boy has learned to read better and recalls a sentence from the book: "Only the unwise think that what has changed is dead."[4] The boy thinks of this quote when he goes home and learns that Sounder has died. He remembers how when he first read the sentence he asked his teacher what it meant. The teacher told him that it meant if a flower blooms once, it will go on blooming for anyone who's seen it. The boy now understands what the teacher meant. Like the stories from the Bible, the quote helps make life bearable. Sounder was alive once and will always live in the boy's memory.

THE BOY'S IMAGINATION

The author effectively uses another narrative technique: he takes us inside the boy's mind and reveals the boy's vivid imagination in response to his encounters with prejudiced white men. In the first instance, the boy is confronted by the man at the jail, and as he looks at his red face and thick neck, he feels the "same total but helpless hatred" he had felt when the men had arrested his father. Curiously, when the boy's father was arrested, we hadn't seen a hateful reaction from the boy—it takes another cruel, prejudiced person to remind him of his earlier reaction:

> He had thought how he would like to chain the deputy sheriff behind his own wagon and then scare the horse so that it would run faster than the cruel man could. The deputy would fall and bounce and drag on the frozen road. His fine leather jacket would be torn more than he had torn his father's overalls. He would yell and curse, and that would make the horse go faster. And the boy would just watch, not trying to stop the wagon....[5]

At the jail, the boy starts looking closely at the cruel man and comes up with a new vision. The man is red-faced, has a big, thick neck, and reminds the boy of a stubborn bull with an enormous neck that he once saw at the big house where his father worked. The bull was in a cattle chute so the animal doctor could vaccinate him in the neck, but the bull was rebelling so intensely that the men put a chain under his neck and hooked it tight. Still the bull insisted on fighting and pushed so severely with his legs that he literally choked himself to death before the men could stop him. The bull collapsed and the chain got lost in the folds of his fat neck. When the chain was released, the bull's head "fell in the dirt, and blood oozed out of its mouth and nostrils."[6]

The boy vividly recalls this and then imagines that the man at the jail, like the bull, collapses and has blood streaming from his mouth and nostrils. While the boy is still upset by this man, there are no more tears in his eyes after he dreams up this image. Wishing the bull's fate on the man makes the boy feel somewhat better. As in the Bible stories he'd heard, in the boy's vision evil reaps death. When he sees his father in the cell, he is reminded of his father's strength and knows his father could easily have choked the man.

Similarly, when the boy is searching on the road for his father and comes across another cruel guard, the author again shows us the boy imagining what could happen to

ON YOUR OWN
ACTIVITY #4

The boy imagines fighting back when he's confronted with the mean guards. What might have happened if he had, in fact, thrown the iron piece back at the guard's head? Do you think he will continue to refrain from fighting back as he grows up? As he becomes more educated, how might the boy become more powerful than such guards without having to physically overpower them?

the man. In this case, the man laughs when the boy's fingers bleed after being hit by a piece of ragged iron. The boy looks carefully at the man, who reminds him of a scarecrow:

> For a second he reminded the boy of a garden scarecrow blowing in the wind, body and head of brown burlap stuffed with straw, the head tied on with a white rag just like the white band around the guard's neck, the head tilting from side to side, inviting a well-placed stone to send it bouncing along a bean row.[7]

Before being injured, the boy had been waiting anxiously for the guarded convicts to stand up rather than hunch over their work, so he could determine if one is his father. But now, after the guard has laughed at the boy being harmed and none of the convicts responded, the boy knows his father is not in the group. He knows if his father had been there, he would have stood up straight to his full height, grabbed the scarecrow man by the neck, and shook him the way the boy had seen Sounder do when he caught a weasel. The boy imagines the man flailing in mid-air as his father holds him by the neck. The man would finally go limp and his father would drop him, as the scarecrow would drop when it was untied from its post and roll away.

The boy's imagination doesn't stop there. When the guard throws another piece of iron at the boy that lands a few feet from him, the boy imagines himself picking up the piece of metal and throwing it at the man. He imagines himself as David striking Goliath. There has been a progression here, then. By this point, the boy thinks not only of how his father could overpower the man but of how he himself could. We feel that the boy is no longer a boy depending on his father but someone who is ready to make his own choices and willing to fight his own fights.

Understanding
the Plot

SOUNDER IS A COMING-OF-AGE STORY, meaning that the plot's main focus is on following the events in the life of one character who is on the brink of becoming an adult and is confronted with all sorts of challenges. Such narratives are written not only for young adults but for adults as well, which shows the broad appeal of this type of writing. Readers of these works see how a young person endures hardships and how circumstances affect how he or she develops. *Jane Eyre* by Charlotte Brontë, *Great Expectations* by Charles Dickens, and *The Adventures of Huckleberry Finn* by Mark Twain are examples of such works.

In *Sounder*, the boy is young when the book opens, but because of events in his life, he is forced to take on adult responsibility and he matures quickly. In the first few pages of the book, some important information is given: the boy looks up to his father; the boy is devoted to Sounder, the family's dog; and the boy has twice tried to get an education. All of these factors will have notable effects on the rest of the plot.

The first significant event in the book, which occurs very early, is that the boy's father is arrested. In the process of trying to help the father, Sounder is shot and so seriously wounded that the boy's mother, and then the boy, believe he will die. When the sheriff and his men come to arrest the boy's father, they are cruel and belittling to the family. It is especially notable that when the men call the father "boy," the young boy mistakenly thinks they are referring to him. This shows how the young boy is unfamiliar with this prejudiced manner of speaking, and it also reinforces how he highly respects his father, never imagining that anyone would refer to him as "boy." The father is handcuffed, tears

ON YOUR OWN
ACTIVITY #5

At the beginning of the book, the boy acts like any other young boy, but by the end, he has taken on adult characteristics. In the beginning, the boy is scared when the men come and arrest his father. If the same men came to his house again at the end of the book and belittled his family, how do you think the boy would respond?

his pants when they get caught on a nail as the men force him into the wagon, and he falls flat on his back when one man pulls on the chain they have attached to him.

The boy worries about his father and what will happen to him, but the father is taken away and the wounded Sounder is still with the boy and perhaps can be helped. The author gives us a detailed description of every effort Sounder makes to move his body, so seriously harmed by the gun, and the author also details the boy's shaken, crying response to seeing his injured dog. Somehow Sounder manages to drag himself under the house. While the boy's mother advises him to leave the dog in peace, the boy cannot do so. He looks under the house for the dog and cannot see him. The boy's head is already sore from when he fell trying to hold Sounder back from the men, but now he squeezes under the house, searching in every corner, and becoming more bruised in the process.

The boy continues to look but has no success, and his mother advises him to stop, since the dog has probably gone to the woods to heal himself with the oak leaves there. Still, the boy searches everywhere he can think of. When the dog finally returns, he is severely deformed; he no longer sounds his loud, distinctive, powerful voice; he has lost his spunk; and he waits forlornly for his master's return.

When authors provide hints to their readers about something that will happen later in the book, it is called foreshadowing. This is what Armstrong is doing in *Sounder*. As the book progresses, we see that the events surrounding the dog's shooting are significant because they hint at what will later happen to the boy's father and how the boy will be affected. Also, however, as the book progresses, the young boy is growing up and changing, so his responses to difficult situations change as well.

The boy sees how the sheriff and his men mistreat his father when they arrest him. The next time he sees his father is when he visits the jail, bringing a cake for his father for Christmas. This turns into another unpleasant experience, again because of a white man's prejudice. On this trip, the boy also sees how disturbing it is to be in the jail, and while he had planned on being pleasant with his father, he finds this impossible. His father realizes how difficult the trip has been and tells him not to come anymore.

Later, the family finds out that the father has been sent to do hard labor and that he may be one of the men who has died working at one of the quarries. They find out, in fact, that he isn't one of the victims, but the boy decides to search for his father or at least for some information about him. After the boy makes many long, nearly fruitless searches, his father arrives home one day. The family learns that he had been trapped as a result of a quarry explosion, but that he was determined to make it home to them. He was released once the jailers realized that he was so harmed by the explosion that he wouldn't be of much use. The father is seriously disabled as a result of the accident; additionally, he seems to have lost his spirit.

By the time the father approaches the family's house, readers can see the parallels between what has happened to Sounder and what has happened to the father. Just as Sounder is badly harmed, physically and psychologically, so is the father. Looking more carefully at what's happened, we also see other similarities between the situations of Sounder and the father. For example, the family members initially thought Sounder was going to die, just as they feared their father had died in the explosion.

Also, there are similarities between the boy's search for Sounder and his search for his father. The boy kept looking for Sounder once his mother guessed that the dog apparently hadn't died but was trying to heal himself. The boy searched everywhere he could think of, getting bruised along the way. Similarly, once the family knew the father was doing hard labor, the boy started to search for him. When the boy decides to look for his father, however, his mother realizes that when her son is determined to do something, he can't be stopped. While the mother has learned from the earlier experience, so has the boy: the fact that Sounder made it home reinforces for the boy that he should never give up searching for his father.

Just as the boy is physically harmed when trying to hold Sounder back and when looking for the dog, the boy is hurt when on the road searching for his father. In both cases, he doesn't let the injuries deter him. When searching for his father, it appears even more important that he not be affected by the injury, since a white guard is laughing at him and taking pleasure in his pain. When the boy searches both for Sounder and his father, he does not find them, but both Sounder and the father eventually make it home on their own. In both cases, the family is not warned of their arrival but sees the wounded one pitifully approaching. For both Sounder and the father, their spirits appear broken and they soon die.

The father's arrest sets into motion all of the previously mentioned aspects of the plot. The plot is purposefully devised so that what happens to Sounder as a result of the arrest is a foreshadowing of what will later happen to the father. The author has circumstances repeat so as to make them stand out even more. Sounder, the father, and the boy do everything in their power to fight the tragic events; from sheer determination, both Sounder and the father survive physically, but we soon realize that they are both seriously harmed emotionally and psychologically as well. Their own inner strength has kept them alive and makes them awe-inspiring, yet ultimately the cruelty of those in authority overpowers them. The plot shows the horror that prejudice causes.

The boy's life is forever altered as a result of the arrest and the plot elements that flow from that arrest. He is forced to take on adult responsibilities, but other changes also occur in him because of these events. For example, because his mother sends him to jail with the cake for his father, the boy is forced to go into the mostly white town and see what jail is like. He is poorly treated by the white guard at the jail, who reduces to crumbs the cake the boy has brought with him. In the boy's mind, he imagines the jailer as the red-faced man and compares him to a mad bull. The boy is specifically remembering a captive bull he saw that fought so hard against getting an injection that he died. Apparently, the boy wishes the same for the jail guard—that he would also die as a result of his own overpowering personality.

By visiting the jail, the boy also gets a perspective on what it is like to be imprisoned. Knowing how the men live there serves as an extra incentive for the boy to search for his father after his father is sent into hard labor. The boy sees that life in jail is miserable, and he is concerned about how his father will be treated outside the prison.

ON YOUR OWN
ACTIVITY #6

Because of the father's arrest, a chain of events takes place. Imagine that the father had never been arrested. What would the young boy's life be like then?

Just as the boy is angry at the jail guard, so he becomes angry with the guard he encounters when searching for his father in hard labor. The boy finds a chain gang working outside and sees how stooped over the men are as they work chained together. The guard laughs when he sees the boy get hurt by a flying piece of metal, yet the boy refuses to let the guard see how much the injury really hurts. He imagines throwing something at the guard himself to harm him. In this case, then, he not only wants the man harmed but wants to do the harming himself, indicating not only his increased anger but that he is tired of not fighting back. He is willing to fight an adult, also indicating that he no longer views himself as only a child.

There are other significant changes in the boy's life as a result of his father's arrest. First, his world is greatly expanded and, second, he begins to get a formal education. The boy's world expands when he first visits his father in jail and then when he sets out looking for his father doing hard labor. We learn that on these trips, he reads signs and also tries to read newspapers that he finds in the trash.

Not only is he learning to read more, but by reading a newspaper the boy is finding out more about the world. He says that the stories in the paper aren't like the Bible stories that his mother tells him, since when he tries to tie together the newspaper stories, they don't have good endings. This also indicates that events are pushing him out of the world of childhood. Mothers typically tell their children pleasant stories, but at some point their children learn that these are only stories and that the world is not as easy or safe as mothers and parents may lead them to believe. The boy has reached this point.

The boy also finds a thick book in the trash and, even though he is unable to read many of its words, he carries it with him, not wanting to give up. This book is partially the reason he gets the schoolteacher's attention when he wanders into a schoolyard in his travels. His injured hand is bloody and he wants to wash it off, but he also wanders into the schoolyard because he's curious about school.

When the teacher sees the book the boy is carrying, he is impressed. He takes the boy home so he can properly bandage his fingers and then reads some of the book to him. Only at this point do we find out what the book is. It happens to be a book of essays by Michel de Montaigne (1533–1592), a famous French essayist who wrote about many issues. The teacher reads the boy a small selection and is so taken by the boy's own life story that he offers to have the boy come to his school; he can stay with the teacher in return for doing jobs around the house.

The author told us in the first few pages of the book how the boy had tried so hard to walk to school each day, so we know how much the boy wants to learn. When he asks his mother if he can accept the offer, she sees it as a blessing from God. Even though the family could use the boy's help at home since the father is still gone, she says the boy should get an education.

At the end of the book, the boy reads to his siblings at home, helping to expand their world as well. We know that as a result of receiving the education and living away from the secluded family cabin, the boy's world will change even further. In the process of searching for his father, the boy has found a great opportunity. If his father had never been arrested and he had not gone looking for him, the boy may have never gotten this opportunity.

■ The unnamed boy is the central figure in *Sounder*. We share what he sees, hears, dreams, and wishes. The arrest of his father and the shooting of Sounder force the boy to journey away from home. On his own, he quickly matures, as he encounters racial discrimination and loneliness but also learns the power of education and religious faith.

■ The big book that the boy discovers in the trash is a book by
Michel de Montaigne (1533–1592), a French essayist who wrote
about the great themes of life. The book proves pivotal to the
story as it brings the boy to the teacher's attention, and the
teacher gives him the opportunity to attend his school.

■ Sounder, the family's hound dog, is named because of his melodious voice. "It filled up the night and made music as though the branches of all the trees were being pulled across silver strings." Both he and the father are severely injured and disfigured in the book because of violence and cruelty. At the same time, Sounder is a tribute to the spirit of life.

■ In *Sounder,* we are reminded of the important relationship that exists between children and parents. The boy looks up to his father and wants to be like him, but his father is taken from him when he is still young. The boy's mother is a great source of wisdom and faith and tries to teach it to the boy. The love and closeness of the family helps them overcome hardships.

■ The setting for *Sounder* is mostly in the isolated home of a very poor family. The family's cabin has a deeply sagging roof, and from the way the boy huddles by the kitchen stove in the morning, we realize that there is not much heat in the rest of the structure. The boy and his family have almost no money, have very little food, are secluded from others, and live in a world of great prejudice. The setting shows us the extreme hardships that the family struggles with day in and day out.

■ In *Sounder*, a key theme is that determination and love help make even the most difficult life bearable. The father suffers when arrested and thrown into the wagon in chains; then he must serve time in jail and later performing hard labor, as in the chain gang pictured here. Only near the end of the book does he return to the family, alive through the power of his own determination.

F

Characters and Characterization

WHEN WE THINK of characters, primarily we think of them as the people in a work of literature. Usually one or more characters are involved in a work; they are doing things and reacting to other characters, to events, or to their own thoughts. However, it is important to think of characters in other ways as well. It is necessary to realize that in literature an author is choosing the characters, choosing how significant or insignificant the characters will be, as well as how simple or complex they will be. All characters have a purpose and contribute to the work's plot, themes, and the development of other characters. As we

27

read, we should think about why a character is in a book—in other words, what his or her function is. Sometimes, when doing this, it is helpful to think about how the work would be different if the character didn't exist.

In *Sounder*, one of the more unusual aspects related to the characters is that they are not referred to by names when they are speaking to each other or when the author writes about them; only the dog, Sounder, is called by name. All of the people, whether in the family or those outside the family that have much smaller roles, are referred to by their place in the family or by some other description ("mother," "woman," or "the red-faced man," for example).

Usually when authors do not name characters, they do so to make the characters appear more universal. In other words, not naming the characters makes it easier for readers to put themselves in the characters' places and therefore be more involved in the narrative. For example, we are not reading a book about a boy named Jonathan Edward III, which might make us assume the boy is rich or from a royal family; we are not reading a book about Jeb, a boy we might assume lives in a rural community on a farm or ranch; nor are we reading a book about Antonio, a boy who might be living in or was born in Italy or Spain, or whose parents are from there. By looking at these examples, we see that names provoke certain responses from us. With *Sounder*, then, we are reading a book about a boy without a name; we do not make assumptions about him based on a name.

Some people who have read *Sounder* have a different perspective on the fact that the characters have no names. Rather than seeing this as a technique that draws readers into the story, they argue that the namelessness makes the characters in the story appear degraded, just as the prejudiced world that they live in has already treated them. This view may be valid, but only in a limited way. It is true that when people assert power over others they may call them demeaning things rather than their own given names. Those asserting themselves view those that they are over-powering as not important enough to have a name. View-ing the namelessness from this perspective would be reasonable if only the powerless people in the book are nameless, but in *Sounder* none of the characters have names (except for the dog), so this technique does not make any characters stand out over others.

THE BOY

In works of literature, the most important character is called the protagonist. In *Sounder*, the oldest boy of the family is the protagonist. He appears throughout the book and, like most protagonists, is different from the other char-acters in the book—he does one or more things that no other character in the work does. When the book opens, the boy, his father, and the family's hunting dog are together on their cabin porch. We are not told the boy's age, but he appears similar to many young boys in that he holds his father in high esteem and likes for his father to treat him as an adult. A small instance of this occurs very early in the narrative, when the boy is on the porch petting Sounder and his father tells the smaller children that they can't come out. The boy enjoys the special treatment. He also likes the fact that his father says he might take the boy hunting with him and Sounder that night if the conditions are favorable.

Immediately in the beginning of the book, we also see how much this boy loves Sounder. We see not only how happy he is just to pet him but how he thinks of and asso-ciates himself with the dog. The boy comments to his father how he and Sounder must be about the same age and how there isn't any other dog like Sounder. While he wants to go to school very much, if he can't, he thinks to himself, at least he can feel good because he has Sounder. The author also tells us how the boy sees characteristics in Sounder that the average person would miss.

So far, the boy appears a typical young boy, caught up in his dog, admiring his father, and not wanting to be seen as a young kid any more. Within the first few pages of the book, though, we realize that he really is not just an average boy. We are told that at the start of school, in two consecutive years, this boy walked eight miles to school each day and eight miles to get back home. After two years, his mother finally told him not to go anymore, as it was such a struggle when the weather turned colder. There is a curious twist here: while parents often have to push their children to go to school each day, here the young boy is the one who wants to go and his mother finally stops him.

From this, the young boy's determination stands out even more. Not only is he willing to walk many miles to and from school each day, but when he stops after his second attempt, the boy thinks how the next year when he tries again he will be older and stronger and the students won't laugh at him for getting there late. Even after two unsuccessful tries, the boy is willing to try again and he believes he will make it on the third try.

It is just such determination that serves the boy so well as the novel progresses. For example, when Sounder is shot and disappears, the boy never gives up looking for him or hoping for his return. Similarly, when his father is jailed, he goes to work to get money for the family. When his employer asks him how old he is, we fear the employer may say the boy is too young to work, but instead he is impressed by how much the boy gets done. With his father jailed, the boy has had to take on added responsibilities but he never complains.

The author writes: "The boy did not remember his age. He knew he had lived a long, long time." In other words, for a young boy he has gone through a lot already, and no matter how difficult the situations have been, he has persevered. Eventually, just as he methodically searched for Sounder after the dog was shot, the boy goes in search of his father when the family hears he has been sentenced to do hard labor. The boy walks for miles, searching for any small word from someone who might have seen his father or who might be able to lead him in the right direction.

Another strong characteristic of the young boy is his care and compassion for his family members and his dog. When his mother leaves him in charge of his siblings, he tells a joke to try to put them at ease. When he sees her returning, he warns them not to pester her, since even though he doesn't know what she's been doing, he assumes it is serious. Similarly, he shows his caring side when he goes to visit his father in jail. His mother warns him not to upset his father with any bad news or dejected spirits, and so, on his trip the boy plans what he will talk about to cheer up his father. Also, when he returns from the trip, he doesn't give his mother too bleak a picture of what it was really like. The boy's compassion also comes through when he searches for Sounder. He himself has been injured but he still pursues the dog. Also, even though it is unpleasant under the house, he crawls to its farthest corners to find the dog so he can help him, tearing his already worn clothes and hurting himself in the search.

We are also repeatedly told that the boy is lonely and

restless, but these feelings are relieved when his mother tells interesting stories. He wishes she would tell more. The boy wants to learn to read so he can find his own stories; he is so interested in reading that he pulls newspapers and books out of the trash to try and teach himself. He assumes that his mother may even have turned down books that were offered to her by the rich folks she works for, and he feels frustrated. As the book progresses, though, we see a determined boy growing up, his strong characteristics becoming even stronger. At the same time, he picks up characteristics of his parents and also gets an education.

THE MOTHER

Another important character in *Sounder* is the boy's mother. She cares for her family very much, is industrious and ethical, and she knows how to get what she needs. When the boy's mother hums instead of singing, it is a sign that she is worried. When she does sing, she usually sings about being on a lonesome trip; at the same time, she, like her son, never complains. She never appears to be angry or frustrated, despite the heartache that the family has endured. The stories she tells her children are stories from the Bible, so we may assume that she gets some of her strength from her religion.

Additionally, she has an understanding of how the world works and a vision of how to best operate in it. When Sounder is shot, she tells her son that dogs usually go away so they can die in peace, and she advises her son to leave the dog alone, telling him he has to learn to let go. Later, when they believe that Sounder has not died, she surmises that he's gone to the woods to use the oak leaves to heal himself, and this proves to be the case.

As the book progresses, the mother seems to know

better when to give her son direction and when to let him find his own way. For example, in the beginning, when she tells her son to leave Sounder alone, she doesn't immediately realize that because the boy is so attached to the dog this is really impossible for the boy to do. Additionally, when she sends him off with the cake to his father and advises that he not upset his father with bad news, while it may be logical advice, it is very hard for the young boy to manage. She tells the boy to be patient while waiting for his father to return. But at this point, she finally realizes she is asking a lot, and as the waiting continues and her son decides he must go and look for his father, she does not try to keep him back.

The boy's mother also is a woman of action. After her husband is arrested, she returns the ham and sausage, hoping this might get the family out of some trouble. When her husband is in jail, she saves money to buy the ingredients to make a cake and gets a box so her son can carry it to him. When they find out that there's been an explosion at the quarry, she finds someone who can read her the newspaper, so they can find out if her husband was one of the ones killed. When they lose the income her husband normally would bring in, she finds more laundry to do so she can make additional money.

THE FATHER

The boy's father worries about feeding his family, is concerned for their overall well-being, is industrious, a good hunter, and understands nature and how to get along in the world at large. In the winter months, when there is no field work to be done, the boy's father hunts with Sounder, who is described as an excellent hunting dog. Yet, when the hunting falls off, the father apparently steals food for his family, only to be caught shortly thereafter, which results in great suffering for him and his family. During the other months, the father works tirelessly in the fields and he even watches for what is growing in the woods—mistletoe and bittersweet—and teaches his son to do so, in order to sell these items in town. When everything doesn't get sold each season, he takes his son from house to house and sells more by making individual appeals.

The father understands the natural world but he also understands people. For instance, when the sheriff comes with his men to arrest him, the father does not fight, knowing that the way society works he would only put himself in greater jeopardy. Similarly, when his son visits him in jail, he sees that the boy is shaken by the experience and tells him to never come back, so he can spare him any further fear and difficulty. Additionally, he tells the boy not to upset his mother by telling her about his whole experience in the jail. When the guard yells for the boy to leave, his father hurries him along, concerned about his safety.

At the very end of the book, the father returns to the

ON YOUR OWN
ACTIVITY #7

In literature, characters interact with each other and help bring out the author's ideas. Some characters exist not so much because they are fully developed personalities we can relate to but because they serve some purpose—for example, to move the plot along and/or to aid or cause problems for the protagonist. In *Sounder*, the father appears on only a few pages yet serves as a powerful force in the book. If the father did not exist, how would the narrative be different?

family, severely harmed from the explosion at the quarry. He symbolizes despair and also determination. He has lost years of his life in jail and doing hard labor and his body is horribly crippled, but he fought with all his power to live so he could return to his family.

SOUNDER

In many ways, Sounder, the family's dog, has a life that reflects his master's life. Like the father, who does what he feels he needs to do for is family, Sounder feels he must help his master when the sheriff and his men arrest the father. While a dog cannot be completely aware of the risks involved in a situation, Sounder knew the men were trouble, and he was determined to help his master. As a result of his concern for the father, the dog is terribly deformed, left with one bad leg, a missing eye and ear, and a disfigured shoulder. While the disfigured father does not return to the family until the end of the book, Sounder returns much earlier, having saved himself (like the father), but he severely misses his master. The fact that he no longer lets out the loud call that made him such a distinctive hunting dog also shows that some of his spirit has been ruined as a result of his experience. He, like the father, is symbolic of what results from the wrath of prejudice—near destruction of body and spirit. At the same time, however, Sounder is a tribute to the amazing, indomitable spirit of life.

OTHER CHARACTERS

The men who arrest the boy's father are symbolic of the horrors of prejudice. Their relatively brief appearance and their actions at the boy's house indicate the depth of their cruelty and inhumanity and the resulting abominable destruction. When they appear at the house, they do not knock at the door but push it in. They yank at the stolen meat so abruptly that it slides off the table and across the floor. They address the father as "boy" to demean him, and they also cruelly announce that they can smell a thief. The father is chained and knocked over onto his back in the wagon. The men warn the boy that they will shoot the dog if he lets it go, and when the boy can no longer hold Sounder back, they do shoot him.

At the jail, the man who lets the boy in to visit his father is also cruel and demeaning. He slams the door in the boy's face and reduces his cake to crumbs and throws it away. He hurries the boy on and makes fun of him.

The teacher who takes the boy in to dress his wounded hand is thoroughly sympathetic and giving. Apparently he is impressed by the boy's story and his great desire to learn to read, but instead of just telling him to come to the school, he offers the boy a place to live in his home. When the boy's mother hears of the teacher's offer, she feels it is a sign that God is looking out for him. Indeed, whether one believes in God or not, it is a chance circumstance that the boy meets the teacher, and the teacher's offer is one of the few positive events in *Sounder*.

ON YOUR OWN
ACTIVITY #8

Sometimes in literature characters experience or do things that average people never have to. During the historical time when *Sounder* takes place, however, what the boy's family goes through was not so uncommon. Imagine you could spend a day with this family. What would it be like? What would you ask the different family members?

The boy's siblings serve to reinforce his own strengths. He is not only older and bigger than them, but he is quite responsible, although he's still very young, which makes him stand out even more compared to how helpless they appear. The siblings do not have individual personalities but seem to exist as another responsibility—they must be fed and taken care of. The mother must take care of them when they are sick, and the boy must watch them if the mother leaves.

The Function
of Setting

THE SETTING FOR *SOUNDER* is mostly in the home of a very poor family. At the beginning of the book, there are so many comments about food and the smell of food that we realize how hungry this family must be. We read that the boy had smelled ham cooking only twice in his life and that in his home pork sausage was only made for Christmas celebration. This helps us sense how poor the family is, and we also see how intense poverty often means not knowing where the next good meal is coming from.

A further indication of how poor the family is comes when the boy watches his mother sewing patches on clothes, apparently a common practice for her. His mother sews patches that stand out from the clothes they're sewed onto. Other young people have made fun of the boy because of those patches and he's been embarrassed, even though his mother has told him not to pay any attention to such comments. Even the family's patches, then, are seen as inferior. At another point in the book, when the boy needs to go under the house to look for Sounder, his mother makes him wear an old coat of his father's. It is described as full of holes.

The family's cabin has a deeply sagging roof. From the way the boy huddles by the kitchen stove in the morning, we also realize that there is not much heat in the rest of the structure. When he describes going to bed, we learn that he must share it with his brother and he can feel the bed slats under him. He is pleased, though, that his mother cleans their sheets as often as she does those of the rich people. This shows her desire to treat her family as best she can.

Outside the cabin, when *Sounder* first opens, it is cold, enough to make the boy shiver. Later, we read, "The wind blew through his clothes and chilled him inside." Not only does the weather remain tough, but this sentence reminds us of how the family has inadequate clothing. The sound of the wind also bothers the boy, who believes the woods should be quiet, knowing he can hear better then. Dim lights cast long shadows outside. "Nothing moved," we read, "except what the wind moved—dead leaves under the cabin, brown blades and stalks from the fields which were dead and ready to be blown away, bare branches of poplars, and the spires of tall pines."[8] Everything is dead and pushed around by the wind. Nature is either brown or bare. Even the tall pine trees, which keep their needles all year, are pushed by the wind. The setting is bleak, but knowing how the seasons progress and that bad weather is usually temporary, we might assume things will get better.

Also, there are no neighbors nearby. We read: "The white man who owned the vast endless fields had scattered the cabins of his Negro sharecroppers far apart, like flyspecks on a whitewashed ceiling." This is the first we learn that the father is a sharecropper, which means he does not own the land he works or the cabin the family lives in. Instead, they rent the cabin from the landowner and the father helps to work the fields for the landowner and receives some of the crop as payment.

Not only does the family live on a farm and therefore outside of town, but even on this farm the family has very little contact with other people, such as the other farmworkers. The description that the author supplies of these separated cabins also may indicate the prejudice of the time. The blacks are separated, perhaps, to discourage them from becoming a united force. They are described as "flyspecks on a whitewashed ceiling." In other words, not only do they mar a clean, white area, but they are seen as insignificant as a common fly.

In *Sounder*, the boy is especially aware of his separateness from others. He frequently feels "night loneliness," especially when the other children are in bed and his father is out. His mother has said it is partially a result of fear, and the boy knows he does not feel afraid when his father is nearby. The boy looks to his mother to enliven his evenings by telling him stories she's heard from the Bible. While the boy finds her stories engaging, he also wishes his mother or father could read. Rather than count on that, he plans to learn to read himself, so he can read his own stories someday.

After the father's arrest and Sounder's getting shot, the

boy is distraught because he does not know what will happen to his father and he cannot find Sounder. The loneliness
that has been a strong mood in the story now intensifies.
The boy's loneliness is described as:

> ... heavier than ever now. It made the boy's tongue heavy.
> It pressed against his eyes, and they burned. It rolled against
> his ears. His head seemed to be squeezed inward, and it hurt.[9]

The loneliness has magnified to such a degree that it is
described as a growing pressure that hits him from all sides.

The book's setting changes when the mother sends the
boy into town with a cake for his father. The boy is afraid
on the road and, as he nears the town, he imagines eyes
looking out at him through curtains in the big houses. He
knows he will see more people as he gets further into town
and is worried that he will be stopped and asked where he
is going or what he is doing with the box.

As he walks, he is happy that no one seems to notice him.
Still, he is afraid of standing out, so even though he is
intrigued by the decorated store fronts and the new toys
inside them, he will only look at them out of the corners of
his eyes as he walks by. He admires the shiny new items
and thinks of the few new toys he and his siblings have
received, as well as the used ones rich people have given
them.

While the town setting is notably different from where
the boy lives, there also is a great contrast when the boy
arrives at the courthouse and has to go around to the back
of the building where the jail is. "The front of the courthouse was red brick with great white marble steps going up
to a wide door. But the back was grey cement and three
floors high, with iron bars over all the windows."[10] In the
midst of the town, the boy wishes he could be back in the

woods, where he's most comfortable. He dreads even knocking on the jail door, and before he is even let inside, there are disturbing sounds coming from inside:

> Somewhere a voice was singing "God's gonna trouble the water." From one of the windows there came the sound of laughter. Now and then a door slammed with the deep clash of iron on iron. There was a rattle of tin pans. The boy felt very lonely. The town was as lonely as the cabin, he thought.[11]

This reinforces the idea that loneliness is not dependent on the number of people surrounding someone but on whether or not there is a connection with any of them. We have all heard people say that in the middle of a crowd they still felt very lonely. This is exactly the boy's reaction to the town. Even though we've learned how lonely he really is, here, in the middle of a town full of people, the boy actually wishes he could be by himself instead.

Once inside and finally walking toward his father's cell, the boy feels many pairs of eyes looking at him, the same reaction he had when walking into town. His steps echo loudly, there is more sad singing, and the author mentions the iron gates and ceiling, cold and forbidding.

The setting is so overpowering and the treatment the boy has received from the guard at the door—who destroys the cake—is so disturbing that the boy and his father have long silences during their visit. The boy has missed his father so much and even practiced the conversation he would have with him, but none of that conversation takes place.

As the boy walks home, the sun dims and he walks in darkness. The houses that he passes are bright, not only with lights inside but also because they have lanterns on their mailboxes to welcome visitors. This stands in contrast to the dim light that was earlier described at the boy's own cabin. The boy feels even more lonely: he is surrounded by people in lovely homes, but he is on his way to a small cabin where there are no visitors.

Later, when the father gets assigned to do hard labor, the situation turns out to be worse for the family, since now they don't know where he is. The boy searches for his father numerous times and rather than just facing the cruel guard at the jail, now the boy is belittled by the guards watching the chained men and by the convicts themselves. Even though the boy had so hated to travel into the town to see his father, once the father is out of the jail, the boy still has the courage to search for him, even though we assume he would rather be in the woods.

When the boy searches for his father, he often travels where he will run into the fewest number of people. At one point, he comes across a school where children are playing on ladders and swings. He is heading for the part of town where the unpainted cabins are. This is where he feels most

ON YOUR OWN
ACTIVITY #9

In *Sounder*, the boy has very different reactions to different places. For example, when he's walking through town by the big houses, he wants to go by unnoticed and hopes no one will stop and ask him any questions. Yet, when the boy walks through a section of a town where the cabins are unpainted, he likes the fact that people talk to him. Similarly, he wants the kind teacher to ask him questions. Explain why this happens. Why should settings create such different reactions in the boy?

comfortable, since the people from such cabins often come out on their porches and talk to him and give him something to eat. Even though he feels the most comfortable with these people, he thinks they may question the reason why he's carrying the big book he's found in the trash. By carrying the book, a sign of education, he no longer fits in where he always has before.

The setting of the school he's just passed is contrasted with the next school he walks near. While the first school had children playing on swings and ladders, at the second school there are no such items. There is a loose drainpipe in this schoolyard and a loose pig that disturbs the children's waiting dogs to such a degree that the drainpipe gets knocked over and mayhem breaks out. The children are allowed to leave school early as a result and rush over to the boy with many questions. It is the first time in *Sounder* he's ever had young people other than his siblings approach him. They are very curious about him and impressed by the big book that he's carrying, but they run off soon after barraging him with questions.

When the white-haired teacher comes out of this school, the boy has good feelings about him. "Now, for the first time in his life away from home, he wasn't feared."[12] The teacher has such a kind demeanor that the boy actually realizes that he wants the man to ask him questions. When the man walks the boy to his house to bandage his injured hand, the setting is different from anything previously described. The man lives in a cabin with a fence and yard, which, in the boy's mind is "almost a big house." Inside the yard, the teacher stops and talks to a plant, which might remind us of how the boy's own father would talk to nature. The boy is at first frightened by the talk but realizes the man is not out of his mind. He asks the teacher what grows on the plant, assuming it must be something special if the man has taken such care with it. But the response is very different from what the boy expects. The plant grows flowers, not food like the plants that would be found around his family's cabin.

The teacher's cabin is different from what the boy knows in other ways as well. He sees that the teacher lights two lamps in the same room, making the room "as bright as daylight," again a strong contrast to the dim light in his family's cabin. The boy also is startled to see two stoves, one for cooking and one for heating, as well as books on the tables and on shelves. "The mellow eyes of the man followed the boy's puzzled glances as they studied the strange warm world in which he had suddenly found himself."[13]

There is a significant difference in the setting at the end of the book as well. The boy and his mother are on the porch at their cabin but it is sweltering hot—a strong contrast to the weather when the book opened. The mother tells him that Sounder has not been acting like himself, as the dog walks back and forth to the road. The mother says he's walked quite a distance down the road and can't settle himself down. She says mad dogs have to get shot before they

ON YOUR OWN
ACTIVITY #10

There is a strong sense of loneliness throughout much of *Sounder*. This intensifies when Sounder and the father are gone. How does the mother help the boy through this? Toward the end of the book, both the mother and boy are singing, a sign that the mood in the book is no longer the same. Why is it different?

bite someone, implying that Sounder may be on his way to madness. The boy calmly tells her that Sounder is fine, just looking for a cool spot.

The mother notices a figure walking in the distance and points it out to the boy. Then she remarks that the catbird near them is agitated for no reason. She says that this is a bad sign, that something bad is going to happen. The boy blames the catbird's reaction on the fact that Sounder probably disturbed her. Again, he is untroubled. Then Sounder lets out his loud call, which has been quiet ever since his master was arrested, and charges down the road. The approaching figure is the father on his way up the road. The boy's untroubled feeling and the mother's troubled predictions both seem appropriate: the father is back but he is horribly crippled. There has been good news and bad, and the setting at the cabin has been changed once again.

Understanding
Themes and Symbols

IN WORKS OF ART, a theme is an idea that the work is presenting; in works of literature, in particular, a theme can be seen as
a message that the author is sending to his or her readers. In
each literary work, there may be one key theme that the author
is presenting, but frequently there is more than one. To determine what the themes are when we read a book, we must ask
ourselves why we think the author wrote the work and what the
author wants us to think about as we read it.

THEMES

In *Sounder*, a key theme is that determination and love help make even the most difficult life bearable. The boy and his family have almost no money, very little food, are secluded from others, and live in a world of great prejudice. Yet, despite these extreme circumstances, their love for each other and continued persistence pull them through. What makes them stand out even further is that no matter what happens, they never complain or lose hope.

Sounder and the father suffer the most physically and psychologically, yet prove to be examples of incredible fortitude. In the beginning of the book, Sounder's striking hunting skill is described as well as his powerful voice, which is said to sound as strong as six dogs' voices. He is vibrant, loyal to his master, and adored by the children in the family. When the father is taken away in chains, Sounder is driven to help him. When Sounder chases after the men, one of them shoots the dog, as the sheriff had warned the boy he would do if the dog came after them.

It is dark, but the boy sees Sounder get shot and knows he must be seriously hurt or dead because the dog does not get up. The boy fears going to the dog to see what's actually happened. Sounder yelps, a striking contrast to his usual strong voice. He stumbles and eventually, with all his

ON YOUR OWN
ACTIVITY #11

Prejudice is severely damaging to all parties. This is one of the themes of Armstrong's book. Describe three examples of prejudice that exist today. Explain how these examples have consequences for those involved and even for those who just hear about the incidences.

might and determination, drags his body under the house, into the farthest corner. The mother says Sounder is preparing to die, but this turns out not to be the case. Instead, Sounder disappears, and despite all the boy's searching, only comes back to the family after he's attempted to heal himself in the woods. It is remarkable that he is alive and could have dragged himself to the woods, since even after some time to heal, he is horribly disfigured—one leg is useless and he is missing part of his head, one eye, and an ear.

The description of Sounder, both when he is first shot and when he later returns from the woods, is heartbreaking. But his will to go on is a testament to his overwhelming determination and strength, the very characteristics that made him try to save the father in the first place. Yet, the dog has not been victorious on all fronts. Sounder no longer uses his voice—what had earlier been one of his key traits—and he seems to have lost his enthusiasm for life, now concerned almost exclusively with his master's return.

What happens to the father is in many ways similar to Sounder's situation. He suffers when the men throw him into the wagon in chains; then he must serve time in jail and later in hard labor. Only near the end of the book does he return to the family and, like Sounder, he is only alive because of his own determination. When an explosion occurred at the quarry where he was working, he ended up trapped under rocks and willed himself to stay alive so he could see his family again. He is pulled out of the rubble and allowed to go home, seriously deformed as a result of his experience. While Sounder is overjoyed to see his master, the father's spirit appears to be broken, and he dies in the woods while hunting, not long after returning to the family.

Sounder's and the father's experiences support the theme that determination and love make survival possible. This theme also applies to the mother's experiences. While she is not physically harmed, she must bring up her children on her own and find other sources of income while her husband is gone for such a long time. The mother also has faith in God, which aids in keeping her determined, strong, and loving.

A similar theme can be found in the boy's story, but it is somewhat altered in his case. Like his mother, the boy does not suffer physical anguish and he also gains knowledge and support from Bible stories. But he suffers emotionally as a result of Sounder's accident and from losing his father for such a long time. He is more lonely and afraid without them. He is also forced to take on adult responsibilities and, as a result of visiting his father in jail and looking for him on the road, he has more personal experiences of racial prejudice.

The boy's experience is unlike all of the other characters' experiences in a significant way. Specifically, by getting an education, his life changes in a way that makes him happier and provides him with the opportunity to live a better life. In other words, while determination and love make survival possible, the author is showing us that learning brings not just survival but growth and opportunity. Within the first few pages of the book, we learn how the boy tried for two years in a row to walk back and forth to school each day— eight miles each way—but finally had to stop when the weather got cold. Still, he was determined to try again the next year.

As the book progresses, we find that the boy has taught himself to read signs and wishes that one of the rich people his mother works for would give the family some of their old books. He thinks his mother would turn down such an offer, indicating how he sees his mother's perspective on reading. He assumes that she would say the family members have no use for books, since they can't read, and that she wouldn't even think they could learn.

The theme of education comes up at other points in the book as well. When the family doesn't know about the fate of his father, the boy thinks of how even if they could get a letter to or from him, they wouldn't be able to write it themselves or read one if their father had someone write back to them. Similarly, when there is an accident at a quarry and they are concerned that the father could have been killed, the mother has to have someone read the newspaper report to her.

During his travels in search of his father, the boy scavenges newspapers and teaches himself more new words. Just by leaving his cabin and looking at these papers, his life has been expanded. When he finds the book of Montaigne's essays, he gets frustrated because he cannot read all the words, but as fits his personality, he still holds onto the book. By not giving up on it, he attracts the attention of the teacher, who knows that the average uneducated person wouldn't be carrying around a large book, let alone one of such tough subject matter.

Of course, the boy's big break comes when the teacher offers to let the boy stay with him and get an education in the school. His mother sees the opportunity as a gift from God, indicating that perhaps all along she has seen the value of education but tried not to concern herself with it, since there seemed to be no realistic opportunities for getting educated. When the boy comes home from school, he's a happier person, proud of his skills, and he reads to his siblings. Even though he hasn't been in school for very long, he is a changed person, and we realize his life will probably be better than if he had followed his father's example and become a sharecropper. All of these elements reveal the theme of the opportunity that education brings.

Also prominent in *Sounder* is the theme of the negative effects of prejudice. While this book focuses on the racial prejudice of whites against blacks, the book's theme can apply to any type of prejudice. The author shows us how prejudice ruins those it is directed against and, at the same time, also ruins those who are prejudiced.

We certainly have an intimate understanding of how the family in *Sounder* is seriously harmed by prejudice. The father is arrested and treated horribly by the sheriff and his men. He finally is released when he is severely crippled as a result of the quarry explosion—no longer useful for hard labor. We wonder how long he would have been in hard labor if the accident had not happened. Also, did the explosion take place because adequate care was not taken in areas where the black convicts worked? There are also serious repercussions for the family because of the father's arrest—Sounder is almost killed, the young boy must take on more responsibility, and the mother's burden increases, since she is the only adult caretaker in a family that was already very poor before the father left.

The author also shows what prejudice does to those who are prejudiced. In this regard, we have a few examples: when the sheriff and his men arrest the father, when the red-faced man at the jail lets the boy in to visit his father, and when the guard by the fence laughs when the boy is injured by a piece of metal. In each case, the racist people treat the blacks in a degrading manner. They seem to see the blacks as beneath them and do what they can to strip them of any self-respect. The irony is that while they see the blacks in this way, they do not realize that their behavior shows that they are not deserving of respect and that they are acting inhuman.

In the beginning of the book, we read of the father's arrest. One of the sheriff's men says he can smell a thief and dramatically pulls the ham off the family's table so that it slides across the floor. The men accuse the father of stealing and cite their evidence, but they never let the father speak or respond to their accusations. At the wagon, they pull on the chain atached to the father's handcuffs, forcing him to fall over. They shoot Sounder in the head. Their ugly actions are certainly not those of responsible legal authorities.

The second example of prejudice occurs when the boy visits his father in jail. The man who is responsible for letting the visitors in is described by the boy as "red-faced" and reminds the boy of a bull. The man is rude, slamming the door in the boy's face. He also destroys the boy's spirit by not just searching the cake he's brought but by reducing it to crumbs. In the first instance of the white and black confrontation, the boy is concerned about his father and dog and the author doesn't describe much of the boy's reaction to the men. At the jail, the boy's reaction is clear: he is angry, and there is a description of him imagining the man as a self-destructive bull. The man is unnecessarily cruel and is dehumanized as the boy imagines him as an angry animal.

In the third example of prejudice, the boy is standing by a fence, once again looking for his father, when a stray piece of iron flies up at him and bloodies the boy's hands. A guard watching the working convicts laughs at the boy's pain. In this instance, again, the white man is cruel and even throws another chunk of metal at the boy. The boy imagines that he could throw the metal back at the guard and harm him. It is the first time in all the situations of prejudice where the boy considers fighting back himself.

This shows that the boy's patience with cruel treatment is wearing thin; perhaps his education and the ever-growing strains that have occurred as a result of his father's arrest have contributed to this. Again, the guard's behavior indicates that he sees himself as being better than the boy, but we realize how the guard sees only a racist image rather than who this boy really is. At this point, we have great respect for the boy in light of what he's gone through—the guard is the one who looks idiotic and base.

SYMBOLS

Aside from themes, works of literature frequently use symbols or symbolism. A symbol is something that stands for something else, and a symbolic action is something that is done to indicate something else. For example, a country's flag is a symbol of the country itself. When people salute the flag, the flag represents their country; they are showing that they honor their country. Similarly, when people burn a flag, it is showing their disagreement with and strong negativity toward that country's policies, leaders, or people.

In *Sounder*, we can see various symbols. How do we know when something is a symbol? Sometimes we know because there is a detail that the author makes a point of drawing our attention to. For example, this occurs when the mother has her son put on his father's old coat when he goes under the house to look for *Sounder*. The coat is symbolic of the father's qualities, of the father himself, and of the fact that the son will soon be forced to put those responsibilities on his own shoulders even though he is so young.

Literally, the mother has the son put on the old coat so that the son's own clothes will be protected. The father's trait as protector remains with the family—even though he is not there, his clothes can provide some help. The fact that the coat is so very large points out how the father's responsibilities are much larger than what a boy should have to handle. Also, the coat is so large that the boy's knee gets caught on it and his head gets yanked down into the dust. This shows again that a father's responsibilities don't properly fit a young boy and, if taken on, will cause him pain.

Other symbols used in *Sounder* are curtains and windows. The mother washes the curtains of the wealthy, white townspeople and the boy appreciates their prettiness. Yet, when the boy goes to town to visit his father in jail, the curtains take on a frightening aspect. As he walks through town, he hopes that none of the white people will take notice of him, so that he won't be asked any questions. But he knows that people can hide behind their curtains and realizes he wouldn't know if they were watching from their windows as he walked by.

The boy thinks about how refreshing it is that outside of the white town none of the cabins, like his own, have curtains. People can look in or out at their neighbors and there is nothing secretive or hidden. We are reminded of the riddle

ON YOUR OWN
ACTIVITY #12

One symbol in *Sounder* is the dog's ear, which the boy finds in the road. We could say that the ear symbolizes courage yet also boyishness. How does it symbolize courage? For example, what happens to the dog after he loses the ear? What does the boy do with the ear? What does he hope to accomplish by doing this? How does this indicate that he is still quite young?

the boy told his younger siblings when their mother left them at home. He says when you're inside you look out and when you're outside you look in—but, he asks, what looks both ways? The answer is a window, and again this riddle reminds us how the boy thinks that the whites, with their curtains covering their windows, are hiding something and are therefore frightening.

The big book that the boy pulls out of the trash also serves as a symbol. The boy tries to read it and is frustrated because he can't, but he still carries it along with him, assuming he will figure it out at some point. The book attracts the attention of the schoolteacher and we then find out what the book is—a collection of the works of the great French essayist Michel de Montaigne. The book, then, is a clear symbol of the boy's determination to learn how to read but also is symbolic of how much there is to know about life.

The book is a collection of pieces describing how one should best live one's life. The book, then, is most appropriate for a boy who's been forced to grow up too quickly and has lost his father to jail and so cannot turn to him for guidance. Most young boys would not be interested in such a book, but we know that this boy is far from average. The teacher readily talks to the boy about the book, showing that the teacher believes the boy's capabilities are strong and can be challenged. The book symbolizes this challenge and opportunity.

Afterword

WHILE READING A BOOK, we are wondering what will happen next and how it will all turn out. By the end, there usually is no longer any mystery about what might happen. When we are done, we should think not just about the ending but also about the earlier events that led to the ending. We should now have a better understanding about how the earlier events fit together, and sometimes they take on greater significance.

In *Sounder*, for example, what happens to Sounder ends up being very similar to what happens to the father. In other words, what happens to Sounder foreshadows, or gives a hint of, the later events in the father's life. Once we are done reading the book, we see this foreshadowing, but we also should reflect on whether it was possible to discern the foreshadowing at earlier points in the book.

Looking back, we realize that once the father is arrested, Sounder and the father are never together again until near the end of the book. At the time of the arrest, Sounder is so horribly harmed from being shot that the mother believes he'll die. Only after the boy does not find the dog's body does the mother, and rightfully so, surmise that the dog must have gone to heal himself and is, in fact, still alive. When Sounder reappears one day unexpectedly, he is horribly deformed from the gunshot wounds but has been strong enough to fight off death.

In the father's case, when he is arrested he is put in chains and pulled down hard into the sheriff's wagon. Just like with Sounder, the family does not know what will happen to him. After the boy's first visit to his father in jail, the family no longer has any news on him. With both Sounder and the father, then, the family is left in the dark and worrying about them. A keen reader might realize that this similarity signals that the two should be compared, although this is a very early clue and perhaps not noticeable.

The family believes Sounder has died but then decides he must be healing himself since they have not found his body. Even so, they are rather shocked when Sounder finally appears and they see his mangled body. In the case of the father, there again are similarities. The mother hears that there has been an explosion at a quarry and she and her son fear that the father may have been killed. Just as the boy searches for Sounder in fear of finding his dead body, the mother finds someone to read her information on the quarry explosion, fearful of the news she may learn. The mother is thankful that the paper does not report that her husband has died in the explosion. At this point, the reader may pick up on the similarity of the two situations—the family thought Sounder was dead but he wasn't and then the family feared the father was dead but he wasn't.

The family is forever hopeful that the father will soon return, but they never think that he may have been harmed in the explosion. Just as Sounder appears unexpectedly and very deformed, so too does the father later painstakingly hobble home unexpectedly and severely crippled. Both also appear to have changed personalities. By this point in the book, then, the similarities between the father and the dog are apparent. And eventually they both succumb to their injuries: the father dies and Sounder follows soon after.

By reexamining the foreshadowing in this book, readers become more experienced at reading closely and can see the care the author took in creating the story. We realize that it isn't only in mystery books that authors give us clues as to what will happen next.

EXPECTATIONS

After finishing a book, it is also helpful to see how similar or different it turned out to be from what we expected before we started reading. Think back to your impressions when you first picked up the book. The cover and title let us know the book would be about a young black boy and his dog. Since the title of the book is the dog's name, we might have expected that more of the book would actually concern the dog than we found to be the case.

When we looked at the cover, we might also have expected that since the boy and the dog are sitting so close the book would explore how this relationship started and grew. Instead, after reading, we know that the relationship was strong but almost completely ruined because the dog was so severely injured. For most of the book, the dog is seriously crippled. Remember that when we first picked up the book, we noticed that the dog and boy were looking in different directions and that the boy had a contemplative or concerned look on his face. Remember that the back of the book warned us that the boy's life would change forever. The quotes from reviewers also reinforced the sadness of the story.

When we initially read that the father was a sharecropper, we might have assumed that the book would have more description of what it was like to work in the fields, but that turned out to not be the case. We might have thought, too, that the farmer who owned the land the family was on might have caused problems for the family or might have been a source of prejudice, but the prejudice comes from elsewhere. We knew the boy's life would be changed, so we probably assumed much of the book would be devoted to him and, in fact, it is.

Another perspective on prejudice in the South, also told from a young person's perspective, occurs in Harper Lee's novel *To Kill a Mockingbird*. In this book, the children that are the main characters are not black, but they learn about the evils of prejudice when their father, a lawyer, defends a black man. Many in the town automatically assume that the black man must be guilty, and they have no understanding of how the children's father could take on such a case. The father tries to shield the children from any harm resulting from the controversy, but this ultimately proves impossible. The children also learn that prejudice is not only directed at people of different races but also at people that others see as different in any number of ways.

Also told from a young person's perspective is Maya Angelou's *I Know Why the Caged Bird Sings*, in which a young black girl and her brother live with their grand-mother and uncle in the South and experience prejudice in many forms. Since their grandmother owns the town's gen-eral store, the children learn much from working there and having contact with so many of its customers, many of whom work in the fields for almost no money. This book, like *Sounder*, also comments about the value of education; both children in *Caged Bird* are smart and do well in school.

In *Caged Bird*, the children are upset when separated from their parents, just as the boy in *Sounder* is rather lost without his father and so concerned about him that he repeatedly searches for him. In *Caged Bird*, no authority comes to take away the children's parents, however—they are divorced, and their mother has decided to leave the chil-dren with their grandmother for the time being. These chil-dren, then, suffer not only because their parents are gone but because they feel their parents don't want them. They

ON YOUR OWN
ACTIVITY #13

Some of the most inspiring characteristics of the boy, his father, and Sounder are their undaunted courage and determination. Stories such as theirs occur not just in fiction but in the real world. Look in newspapers or magazines for stories of real-life heroes, or ask someone you know if they know a true story where a person displayed such courage. Imagine that you could interview a person from one of these stories. Write that interview.

struggle with feelings of abandonment and become insecure. As in *Sounder*, however, they learn courage from their elders, in this case their grandmother, mother, and other relatives.

There are many books with characters who show great courage in the face of great challenges. Authors hope to inspire us with such stories. When we read them, we feel not only inspired but reminded that we may underestimate ourselves, that we have more capacity for greatness than we suspect. Often we think of fiction books as a method of relaxation or an escape from our own lives, but authors of books such as *Sounder* also want to make us think and learn.

PREJUDICE

Sounder's author makes us think about prejudice. We have probably heard about it on the news or maybe, unfortunately, seen it displayed in our own schools or neighborhoods. What causes it? To a large degree, it seems to be based on a lack of knowledge. Who or what is different from us makes us uneasy and even fearful. Think of the first time you went to a new school, petted a big dog, or jumped in a swimming pool. You really had no idea of what these experiences were like until you tried them. Similarly, people often have misconceptions about people that are unlike them or that they don't know. Unfortunately, when these misconceptions persist and fear mixes in, serious problems can ensue. To combat this, more and more schools, organizations, and communities sponsor tolerance programs that are designed to defuse prejudice and prevent its escalation.

In *Sounder*, characters suffer not only because of acts of prejudice that take place in the book but also because of the loneliness and separation that the prejudice causes. This is something we may not think about so much when we hear stories of prejudice in our own lives. When a group is not accepted by the main population, it is alienated. Those in the alienated group constantly are on the outside. Think about how this happens in schools where there are social groups that don't let others in. Or think of how hard it sometimes is to be accepted when you move to a new school or new neighborhood. Eventually, people usually manage to make friends, but what happens when they don't, when they seem to never be accepted? Violence at schools, unfortunately, has often been done by students who were loners, who felt unpopular, or who thought they were "losers."

CHILDREN AND PARENTS

In *Sounder,* we are also reminded of the important relationship that exists between children and parents. The boy looks up to his father and wants to be like him, but his father is taken from him when he is still young. As a result, the boy feels even more lonely and abandoned than he had before. In our own society, we see the negative effects on children that have missing parents, whether through

ON YOUR OWN
ACTIVITY #14

In *Sounder,* the family suffers greatly because of prejudice against them. Today, various groups work to help people be more tolerant. Choose one such group and report on how it accomplishes its tasks and what it does in its educational efforts.

divorce, abandonment, death, or time in prison. The person left to raise the child has to take on more responsibility and often has to find ways of increasing income; usually this means that he or she is away working more often. Children may be left on their own to a greater degree and must cope with feelings of abandonment.

Sounder also shows us a successful single parent. The boy's mother is a great source of wisdom. She has great faith and tries to teach it to the boy. She tells him Bible stories, and he always wants to hear more. In our own time, we know there are plenty of single parents who make great sacrifices to bring up their children and that their children often go on to succeed in life.

THE BOOK'S TITLE

When we are done reading a book, we should also think about why the author chose the title. The title of *Sounder*, of course, reminds us of the importance of the dog in the book and his relationship to the boy. We have seen how much the boy loves the dog and the importance of having Sounder in his life. When Sounder gets shot, the boy does everything in his power to find him. The dog, in turn, is quite devoted to the boy and the father.

You probably know many people who have pets, or perhaps you have pets at home. Many people become quite attached to their pets, and their pets become attached to their owners. Pets can make people happy and are an aid for people who are sick and for older people. Pets can also teach children and young adults responsibility. As young people grow up and go through a stage where they feel misunderstood, they may feel comforted by pets that remain loyal to them. In fiction and nonfiction, there are many stories of pets looking out for or saving their owners.

Sounder reminds us of the strong bond that is possible between animals and humans.

ACCEPTANCE

Another key element in *Sounder* is the fact that the family accepts what it cannot change, while fighting on all other fronts. When the father is arrested, the family does not fight back with lawyers or protests. The mother instead tries to return the food that the father has been accused of stealing. Similarly, the boy tries to make himself unnoticeable on the street when he has to walk into the white town. He does not fight back with the guard in the jail or the guard by the hard-labor workers. The mother and boy work as hard as they can to make up for the lost income once the father is taken away. The boy grows up and never complains about any extra responsibilities. He continually searches for his father, regardless of how difficult it is to do so.

This same acceptance is shown when death occurs in the family. When the father dies in the woods, no one is emotionally distraught. The death is accepted as something natural that had to happen. The mother, quite practically, even manages to put money aside so the father can have a proper burial. The father, too, seems to have accepted his death: one wonders if he knew he was going to die and went to the woods since that was his favorite place. When Sounder brings the boy to his dead father, the father is there, still with his light beside him, almost as if resting. Death seems to have come quite naturally.

Similarly, after the father dies, the boy digs a grave for Sounder and predicts that the dog will soon die. Again, quite practically, he knows he will be away from the family while at school and doesn't want his mother to have to dig a grave in the cold, hard ground. This reaction is quite different from how he felt when Sounder was shot. Today, many people in our society comment on our lack of connection with the natural world and our desire to have things our own way. *Sounder* shows us the value of learning to accept what is not in our control and of fighting for what we can change.

Study Is Hard Work (1956)

The Peoples of the Ancient World (1959), co-authored with Joseph Ward Swain

87 Ways to Help Your Child in School (1961)

Tools of Thinking: A Self-Help Workbook for Students in Grades 5–9 (1968)

Sounder (1969)

Word Power in 5 Easy Lessons (1969)

Barefoot in the Grass: The Story of Grandma Moses (1970)

Sour Land (1971)

Hadassah: Esther the Orphan Queen (1972)

The MacLeod Place (1972)

The Mills of God (1973)

Through Troubled Waters (1973)

The Education of Abraham Lincoln (1974)

My Animals (1974)

Joanna's Miracle (1977)

The Tale of Tawny and Dingo (1979)

Study Tactics (1982)

Study Tips: How to Study Effectively and Get Better Grades (1990), co-authored with M. Willard Lampe II

A Pocket Guide to Correct Study Tips (1997), co-authored with M. Willard Lampe II and George Ehrenhaft

1. William H. Armstrong. *Sounder*. New York: HarperTrophy, 1969, p. 26.

2. Ibid., p. 90.

3. Ibid., p. 97.

4. Ibid., p. 114.

5. Ibid., pp. 59–60.

6. Ibid., p. 61.

7. Ibid., pp. 86–87.

8. Ibid., p. 16.

9. Ibid., p. 31.

10. Ibid., p. 56.

11. Ibid., p. 58.

12. Ibid., p. 93.

13. Ibid., p. 97.

Armstrong, William H. *Sounder*. New York: HarperTrophy, 1969.

Nevins, Allan, Henry Steele Commager, and Jeffrey Morris. *A Pocket History of the United States*. New York: Simon & Schuster, 1986.

PinkMonkey Literature Notes on *Sounder*. *http://pinkmonkey.com/search armstrong.asp*, 1997.

Robbins, Mari Lu. *A Guide for Using* Sounder *in the Classroom*. Westminster, CA: Teacher Created Materials, 1994.

Gaines, Ernest J. *The Autobiography of Miss Jane Pittman*. New York: Dial Press, 1971. Set in rural Louisiana, this book looks at 100 years of history, as seen by a black woman who was a child at the end of the Civil War and lived to see civil rights advances in the 1960s.

Gipson, Frederick Benjamin. *Old Yeller*. New York: Harper, 1956. As in *Sounder*, the boy in this story lives in the country not so long after the Civil War. He too must take on adult responsibilities and suffer when circumstances turn bad for his dog.

Hakim, Joy. *Liberty for All?* New York: Oxford University Press, 1994. This book, written specifically for young adults, discusses the lack of universal liberties in the rapidly expanding nineteenth-century United States.

Naylor, Phyllis Reynolds. *Shiloh*. New York: Atheneum, 1991. A young boy in West Virginia must decide what to do when he is confronted with a beagle that has run away from an owner that mistreats it.

Rawlings, Marjorie Kinnan. *The Yearling*. New York: Scribner's, 1938. Living a hard life in inland Florida, a young boy wishes for a pet and befriends a fawn, which brings him happiness but also teaches him tough lessons about life.

Rawls, Wilson. *Where the Red Fern Grows: The Story of Two Dogs and a Boy*. Garden City, NY: Doubleday, 1961. Set in the Ozarks area of Oklahoma, this is the tale of a boy and his two hound pups. They become skilled hunters, winning a hunting award and even taking on a mountain lion, with tragic results. .

page:

A: © Bettmann/CORBIS

B: © Bettmann/CORBIS

C: © Kirsten Soderlind/ CORBIS

D: © Getty Images

E: © Bettmann/CORBIS

F: © Bettmann/CORBIS

cover: © Bettmann/CORBIS

PAMELA LOOS has written and/or researched more than 40 books about literature, covering a range of authors and works. She is a certified English teacher